KEN SIBANDA

The Tragic Circumstances of 1948

A Play in Three Acts

Written by

KEN SIBANDA

In 1948, the National Party came into power in South Africa, solidifying the Apartheid system.

The Tragic Circumstances of 1948 is a play and work in historical fiction. Names, characters, places, and incidents are the product of the author's imagination or are used fictitiously. Any resemblance to actual events, locales, or persons, living or dead, is entirely coincidental. This play may not be performed by prior permission of the copyright owner.

Proteus Books, A Division of Proteus Films

P.O. Box 32, Creswell, North Carolina

Copyright © 2011 Kissinger Nkosinathi Sibanda

Published in United States by Proteus Books, A division of Proteus Films

1. Plays – South Africa.   2. Apartheid.   3. Racism.

4. Race Relations – Fiction.   5. Drama.   I. Title.

Library of Congress Control Number: 2011920826

ISBN 13: ISBN 978-0-9886156-3-2

ISBN 10: 0988615630

LC 2015932155

Printed in the United Stated

First Edition

Contact Publisher: publisher@proteusfilm.com

For my wife,

Charmaine.

The Tragic Circumstances Of 1948

KEN SIBANDA

Other works by Ken Sibanda

Plays

Hannibal the Great

Anthology of Poems

The Songs of Soweto

If God was a poet

Fiction

The Return to Gibraltar

Non-fiction

Lemba Jewish Rights

Building Bridges Confronting the Gap between Black Africans and African Americans (Co-author)

DRAMATIS PERSONAE

TONY MZILA......................Semi affluent café owner.

JACK van RUNSEEN............A policeman with the South African Police.

JOHNY CRONJE.........................A policeman with the South African Police.

THANDEKA DANZILE...An actress

NED QABA...A lawyer

MAMA QOBOZA...Chabeen Queen (club owner)

Mr. PIENAAR...........................Diligent State PIENAAR in the office State

Mr. JOSEPHINEINE WOODWARD...............MAGISTRATE WOODWARD in the Municipal of Simon's Town, the heart of the South African Naval community.

The action takes place at TONY's Café shop in Simon's Town, Cape Town - a meeting place for a host of characters; and a MAGISTRATE WOODWARD's court in downtown Simon's Town.

ACT I SCENE I

Narrator:

With the defeat of the Zulu at Ulundi in 1879, and the Xhosa war of 1779-1879 in the Cape, the 100 Years war, South Africa fought bitterly for self rule. This struggle would resume again when Apartheid tightened its bitter grip ...on the African.

NEWSREEL OFFSTAGE ROLL: News from Government House, Pretoria, where the National Party has come to power through a landslide. The NP has vowed to continue with the policy of Apartheid and segregation.

At wake.

The sounds of *mbaqanga* music (drums and flutes play) floats on stage; a movable empty transportable cafe, two police men of the South African police walk in. A shaky looking canteen that has signs of Coca-Cola, white South African models and Union flag of the old South Africa. The two police officers take a seat next to each other. And turn their backs on the Canteen.

VAN RUNSEEN: *Ya, menieer* (with a heavy South African Afrikaner accent), so this is the place you were talking about

CRONJE: It just opened,last week I believe.

*The café owner, **TONY MZILA**, walks in. He is the town businessman, a man who does his own café management. He ignores the two policemen and starts fixing his bar. Mzila is dressed in a patriotic colored shirt.*

RUNSEEN: Ha boy, how long....

MZILA: (ignores him)

RUNSEEN: Do you see this, when you are nice to them they act like they are kings ....

CRONJE: Or Queens...

RUNSEEN: Hey, comrade....how long this place open boy?

MZILA: (raises his fingers)...Two

RUNSEEN: Two what?

MZILA: You guess minner'...

CRONGE: Don't give me lip!

MZILA: Its not lip, its words coming from my lips ....two weeks.

CRONJE: If it's not lip, what is it then?

MZILA: Nothing!

CRONJE: Okay., give us some coffee and toast, can you do that?

MZILA: I can do it....

CRONJE: (*to Runseen*)Very cheeky bastard! This new law will fix them...

RUNSEEN: The new law by the National Party?

CRONJE: Yes, tell me about it. Hey, let's have some water please!

RUNSEEN: It's a new law that will put the Bantu in his place for once.

CRONJE: Put him in his place?

RUNSEEN: No more mixing with the Bantu – he will have his own hole where he can live and the white Man will have his own place. It's in line with the Bible really! Somewhere in the Bible it says that races should not mix!

CRONJE: Do you exactly where in the Bible, this is said...

RUNSEEN:I would imagine in the New Testament... Timothy perhaps!

CRONJE: What about the Old Testament?

RUNSEEN: No...no....I don't believe this law came before Jesus arrived.

CRONJE: Jesus arrived!

RUNSEEN: You make him sound like a car?

CRONJE: I meant, when Jesus came to earth, that's what I meant.

RUNSEEN: Your view of the world is very biblical ....

CRONJE: I was raised a very strong Christian – Dutch reformed church.

RUNSEEN: Let's leave religion for another day. When two people argue, religion will always set them apart. Okay, let's raise a toast --- to, no religious argument.

CRONJE: But is the position of the Nationalist Party, - the ruling party – not a religious position?

The two stare at each other.

Enter Nomdiphelo Danzile, a beauty queen of the township, she aspires to be an actress. The two policemen and Mzila stare at her. Mzila greets Nomdiphelo in Xhosa.

MZILA: Molo, Noma

NOMDIPHELO DANZILE: Eta Mzala! The usual egg sandwich and fruit juice.

MZILA: Uphuma ku- show. Bekunjani? *You just came from the theater, how was it?*

NOMDIPHELO: Hayi bo, - *No, today we rehearse in the afternoon..*

MZILA: *Richard the III...*

NOMDIPHELO: *Yes, very much so...King Richard.*

MZILA: *When are you going to do plays about South Africa, by and for South Africa. Written by and acted by South Africans.*

NOMDIPHELO: *You know we can't do that, we will get arrested, and we are banned from doing any South African material..*

MZILA: *But....some white South Africans have written and produced material...*

NOMDIPHELO *(looking at the two police officers): No politics today Mzila. Just the sandwich and fruit juice!*

RUNSEEN: Yes, just give the lady some fruit juice and sandwich. and stop talking nonsense.

MZILA: *It's not nonsense!*

RUNSEEN: *Be careful boy...*

MZILA: (whispering to NOMDIPHELO:)These bloody police men!

RUNSEEN: *What did you say yaw!*

MZILA: I said, I wish I could make ...bloody maries here!

RUNSEEN: *Be careful!*

NOMDEPHELO: *Thanks., see you later, by the way I forgot to ask how is George!*

MZILA: George is good, he writes....

THANDEKA: As long as he writes that's good! Chow!

CRONJE: *That's a cutie pie...*

RUNSEEN: I never give the Bantu women a second look chana*!*

CRONJE: Some of them are beautiful.

RUNSEEN: Still there are not blonde and blue eyed!

CRONJE*(laughing):* But Jack, no one in your whole bloody family is blonde and blue eyed!

RUNSEEN: What you laughing?

MZILA: Blonde and blue eyed ha?

CRONJE: How long does it take to get coffee and toast in this café; if it's not ready, we will take you down town under the new law boy!

RUNSEEN: Yes, since I been here you have been talking nonsense; complete nonsense!

MZILA: Get out of my café!

RUNSEEN: Okay, you asking for it, you are officially under arrest, ya.

MZILA: I don't café if it's official or un-official just leave.

CRONJE: What about our coffee and toast?

RUNSEEN: Screw that, just arrest the block.

MZILA prepares himself to be arrested and confidently leaves with the policemen. He offers no resistance.

ACT I SCENE II

MAGISTRATE WOODWARD WOODWARD enters the court and the defendant, **MZILA** is led in; State by Mr. **PIENAAR** is on one side and the defendant is unrepresented. This resembles Old Bailey Criminal Court in London but has neither the calm nor the sophistication of the Victorian era. It's Old Bailey in the sticks.

MAGISTRATE WOODWARD WOODWARD: (Looking through the material): How do you plead, Mr. Tony Mzila to the charge of resisting arrest with intent to commit a riot.

MZILA: Not guilty.

PIENAAR: We would like to present the case right away your honor and save the State valuable time and money.

MZILA: I am entitled to an attorney, may I have my attorney represent me?

MAGISTRATE WOODWARD WOODWARD: Look Mzila. You got yourself in a lot of trouble here ya, I heard about this case; now tell me why did you not want to make coffee for these officers.

PIENAAR:...and toast!

MZILA: It's a long story

MAGISTRATE WOODWARD: You are obviously not taking this seriously. *(motions with finger)* I have all the time

PIENAAR: He is a cheeky fellow this one....like your Jabavu!

MAGISTRATE WOODWARD: Really, is he another Jabavu!

PIENAAR: Oh yes your honor. Big things have small beginnings, as Janie (Jan Smuts) said, in his book – HOLISM, there is no place for the African to exist in...

MAGISTARTE: Ok, that's enough, I get your point. Do you have evidence of his involvement in anti-establishment activities and subversive activities.

PIENAAR: Not really your honor, but two seconds with the fellow is enough.

MAGISTRATE WOODWARD: Maybe PIENAAR should stick to one case at a time; inciting riots and treason allegations are very serious - Mr. Greenwood.

MZILA: I have a lawyer and would like to be represented in this matter.

MAGISTRATE WOODWARD: Where is your lawyer?

MZILA: NED Qaba

MAGISTRATE WOODWARD: Look, Mzala, don't turn this into a political matter, the new law is clear in this very clear, you are to play second fiddle to the whites, got it. In fact section three says, I quote;

MZILA:(Silence) Is this a political trial?

MAGISTRATE WOODWARD: Got it!

MZILA:(silence)

PIENAAR: Your honor, this man is an ambitious politician pretending to be a café owner?

MAGISTRATE WOODWARD...Or maybe He just has bad hearing..

PIENAAR: Maybe….

MAGISTRATE WOODWARD: Look Mr. Mzila, I have done my best to accommodate your shenanigans, the State finds probable cause and we will hear opening testimony next week. In the mean time I advise you as a christian and friend to not follow in the footsteps of these ANC fellows! Education for the Bantu!

MZILA: Thank you for the advice….but I will remain uneducated under this system.

MAGISTARTE WOODWARD: Look….I am charging you in contempt, and fining you $200 Rands.

MZILA: Thank you…

MAGISTRATE WOODWARD: Make that $300 -

PIENAAR: …we are dealing with an element here your honor!

MAGISTARTE WOODWARD:(getting up)Or just a fool with a lost cause…Mr. Mzila please don't rock the boat!…., you turned my courtroom into a bloody circus *ya,* a bloody circus.

MZILA: It was already a circus before I got here!

MAGISTRATE: Okay, the State can proceed… be careful Mr. Mzila that you don't come across the wrong way!

PIENAAR: Your honor due to the disrespect the defendant has shown you I request the defendant be held without bail and under the new section 22 provision.

MAJISTRATE: Motion is granted

Township music plays (Mbaqanga) as players exuent.

ACT I: SCENE III

Later that day the **MAGISTRATE JOSEPHINE WOODWARD**, and the PIENAAR meet outside the court house. ENTER **MAGISTRATE WOODWARD** followed by **PIENAAR**.

PIENAAR: If I could a word with you, your honor.

MAGISTRATE WOODWARD: Yes... what is it, you know that this is very unprofessional

PIENAAR: Yah I know, but we have to stick together you know.

MAGISTRATE WOODWARD: I am well aware of the new government's approach to these matters... what is it?

PIENAAR: I think we have to set an example with this one –

MAGISTARTE WOODWARD: And why so....why him, after all the fellow is just a café owner. This law makes us vindictive.

PIENAAR: He is one of those following Jabavu, the ANC, the resistance to the laws.

MAGISTRAE WOODWARD:. Ya Jabavu, come on, you already failed to prove the link.

PIENAAR: I know he is an ANC follower, I can feel it in my bones.

MAGISTRATE WOODWARD: Don't tell me you can taste it in your blood as well.

PIENAAR: (disdainfully) Not quite.

MAGISTRATE WOODWARD: Then what?

PIENAAR: This fellow has to be cut down to size...

MAGISTRATE WOODWARD: Or rained in I would imagine.

PIENAAR: Call it, what ever you will but the fellow is rocking the boat, I hear that there is already brewing a campaign to free the man.

MAGISTRATE WOODWARD: Then would it not work in your favor, to not have him imprisoned; then there is nothing to free clearly. This man is not another Luthuli. He just does not want the police sitting in his café and drinking coffee, going on... I don't blame the chap actually.

PIENAAR: We cannot afford this charismatic element on the street....

MAGISTRATE WOODWARD: I see..(annoyed)..anything else, I have to go for my tennis appointment. I have no more time for this, if the government's position is that we have become a military State, then it should be prepared for an onslaught from the blacks.

PIENAAR: I beg your...

MAGISTRATE WOODWARD: You heard me MR ahh. ..whats your name again...

PIENAAR: Pienaar

MAGISTRATE WOODWARD: Mr. Pienaar,...yes, what would you do, if you were a black person. Would you not fight for your freedom? And I thought a black middle class is a good thing for blacks!

PIENAAR: Maybe, and maybe not...this has nothing to do with me... I don't make the laws, I an an enforcer.

MAGISTRATE WOODWARD: The national party is trying to corner the black Man but the result will be disastrous I tell you....we are out numbered in this country. Why not leave the Mzilas alone and focus your attention to the real source.

PIENAAR: Just whose side, are you on?

MAGISTRATE WOODWARD: The white side!

PIENAAR: You sound more like an advocate of the Bantu; the Luthuli's and Jabavu.

MAGISTRATE WOODWARD: That's because you see things differently...the law can be racist as you may wish...but it still has to have a minimum amount of integrity. It should be believable for Christ sake. And enforced in a manner that's fair to the Bantu.

PIENAAR: Unbelievable....

MAGISTARTE WOODWARD: Yes, our sentences will not survive appeal if the trial is littered with unsound evidence. Let's just stick to the evidence and facts Pienaar.

PIENAAR: But the law says....

MAGISATRATE WOODWARD: The law says its time for my weekly squash match....see you next week, better have something for me on this case or else I will through it out. No political mambo jambo. The evidence Pienaar; the evidence Mr. Pienaar. And remember law school - - *chana*, the law is an ass.....**Exeunt players.**

ACT I: SCENE IV

Outside the **MZILA**'s café; the town lawyer **Ned Qaba** arrives looking for Tony. He whistles... A tall skinny looking fellow of reputable intellect.

He looks around.

NED QABA: Come on Mzila, where are you, it's almost Theree?

QABA enters the café...

NED QABA:(looking)He looks around, where are the papers, we need them for the newsletter, where did he put them.

Arriving, an elderly AFRICAN WOMAN OF SOME SOCIAL BEARING.

MAMA QOBOZA: Did you hear Mzila was arrested for not preparing coffee and toast for the two policemen?

QABA: When?

MAMA QOBOZA: This morning...The policemen asked specifically for toast with jam and I believe..somke coffee and when they came back he just starred at them like an angry dog.

QABA: How suka la....kutwa iarrengitwe lento. This does not sound like the Tony I know.

MAMA QOBOZA: They took him to the station for processing..

QABA: What is he charged with.....did they find anything on him...

MAMA QOBOZA: He is in violation of the new law.... No they did not find anything (looking up) Thank God! No...not that I heard of, but you know the police, always come later and search the place; what papers are you talking about.

QABA: Political writing... , this is a police State, a Nazi State I tell you. A man can be charged with reading "The Economist."

MAMA QOBOZA: I thought you were not interested in politics....just a lawyer ha?

QABA: It's a long story....

MAMA QOBOZA: Go ahead I am listening, I remember you when you were a law student, no one studied like you, every minute my boy ..always reading...you know what they called you.

QABA: Professor!

MAMA QOBOZA: Professor of laws with an "s" at the end. Anyway, what papers - don't get yourself in trouble after all this hard work now as a lawyer.

QABA: I won't.....the papers I have to find the papers..

QABA runs out. Drum rolls.

MAMA Qoboza: (in a soliloquy) Ohh Mzi my love, just when things were starting to be different between us.

She EXITS.

NED QABA re-enters again...

NED QABA: I got to find the papers....(yells ouward to the side as if seeing at a distance) mama Qoboza wait.

At a different part of twon. The two QABA and QOBOZA catch up. Re-enter stage.

MAMA QOBOZA: What does the new law say?

MAMA QOBOZA: I don't know, but I think it says something like you have to prepare coffee and make toast when the whites tell you to do it.

QABA: Is it a coffee and toast law...like the Americans had?

MAMA QOBOZA: I don't know anything about America, I am born and bread; the only America I know is Humprey Bogart.

QABA: Humprey Bogart....

MAMA QOBOZA: What is a coffee and toast law.

QABA: I will tell you one day..but for now, I must attend to Mzila, I have to help him, he was good to me when I was a law student...

MAMA QABA

I never forget, you did us proud son of Qama.

QABA: Ewe mama, ndibaphethile! (hit the nail on the nail)

MAMA QABA: Go and see Mzila, tell him we love him...tell him that we are behind him.

QABA: I will and when I get back I will tell you about the coffee and toast laws in America...

MAMA QOBOZA: You better...One other thing of some importance – when Mzala was being arrested he said to the policeman; you will pay for this!

QABA: No he didn't

MAMA QOBOZA: Or yes he did!

QABA: That's subversive activities and terroristic Threats, he should have known better! I gotta see Tony...

QOBOZA: They are holding him downtown, at the Capetonian Court yard; for processing.

QAMA: Was it a peaceful arrest?

QOBOZA: Yes...Tony, did not offer any resistance. Siva ngaBantu. (what people are saying.) Okay I'm gone, tell me something. What business do you have with Mzila ha? I have seen you here rather regularly. On a regular basis.

QABA: I and Tony (almost reveals)... just friends!

MAMA QOBOZA: Just friends?

QABA: Yes...And I thought man and woman cannot be just friends.

QOBOZA: Tony is different. A different man and woman can just be friends.

QAMA:*(Inquisitively)* Okay just a friend huh!

QOBOZA: Yes, friends for life....

QAMA: Sounds like the union of South Africa, are you sure you are not Tony's new wife.

QOBOZA: Come on Ned, a woman like me with Tony - you have lost your mind.

QAMA: Lost my mind, we will see, the Greek gods said opposites, attract do you know that Zeus the god of fire was terribly attracted to Achilles... they say it was the collision of fire with water. One element is extinguished as a new one is created. Also my experience as a lawyer is that the greater and louder the denial, the more plausible the result.

QOBOZA: Only in South Africa can a black man talk so knowledgeable about Zeus with close to no knowledge of our heroes – you are very poetic! Faku, Shaka, familiarize yourself with our local history to be truelly great Qama.

QAMA: (brushing it aside) What is your point ma? Greatness is not a part of my agenda.

QOBOZA: If you say so. No point, just an observation.

QAMA: You have a quick mind for someone who is just a chabeen queen?

QOBOZA: Don't call me that.

QAMA:What...

QOBOZA:Chabbeen queen..I am a hostess.

QAMA:Hostess!

QOBOZA:Yes, any way I have to go, say hi to Tony for me. When you see visit him in jail.

QAMA: You can say hi to him when you see him yourself!

Exeunt players. Silence.

A voice over: A man sits in jail for refusing to serve his masters. That man is Tony Mzila. I write to you mama from prison to take care of my children, the café, and my beloved Maria Qoboza.

A revolutionary song is heard behind stage:

O safu saphel' isizwe simyama.

ACT II: SCENE I

A pudgy police officer sits in an office processing papers. QAMA enters and sees the officer. The two stare at each other.

QAMA: I am here to see Mzila.

JAILER : Mzila?

QAMA: Yes, TONY MZILA

JAILER : What business do you have with him boy.

QAMA: I am his attorney!

JAILER : Attorney...stop lying, what you really want. I will have your ass locked up for civil disobedience, now what do you really want.

QAMA: I already told you, I am his attorney.

JAILER : Okay you are just asking for it boy! There are no black attorneys in South Africa.

QAMA: ...huh

JAILER : First let me see your license –

QAMA: (Searches one pocket after the other)..Now where is that license..

JAILER : Maybe you never had it to begin with?

QAMA:..Oh here, (giving it)

JAILER : You sure this is not a fake a forgery. I am going to make a phone call and if this is fake I am locking you up on the spot, you hear me boy.

QAMA: It's real...make the phone call.

The Jailer walks away and makes a phone call. Comes back – (we hear the clicking of a phone line) JAILER returns to stage.

JAILER : (Disappointed)...Mr. **Ned QAMA**, attorney at law - excuse me. How come no one tells me we have a Bantu attorney, ha?

QAMA: Now can I see Tony

JAILER : you have 15 minutes, do you have your notice of appearance pursuant to the criminal procedure act.

QAMA: (taking it out of his brief case) Here...now go and get Tony, I have heard enough of your games –

JAILER : Be careful, you are an attorney but in the eyes of the law you are still a Bantu, don't rock the boat.

JAILER goes out and brings in **TONY MZILA**.

JAILER : 15 minutes, let me search you!

QAMA: Is that all, (to Tony) How are you, you look like you lost weight.

MZILA: I'm fine...just a bit tired.

QAMA: One day of jail and you lose weight. I guess prison diet is not gourmet?

MZILA: (laughing) Gourmet!

QAMA: Nice...delicious...well cooked.

MZILA: No it's not gourmet (laughs)

QAMA: Let's get to your case, some preliminary facts. You are charged under the new law for engaging in actions against the government, statute 1948 section 62. It says that...anyone knowingly engaged in subversive actions against the government's guilty of the crime of treason and here this section, see section 22 – inciting a riot.

MZILA: Treason! Wow, I only refused to save the bastards some coffee and toast.

JAILER : Watch your language kaffir? (looking at the two. The two men ignore him).

QAMA: What else!

MZILA: That's all..

QAMA: (thinking Why did they come after you so hard!

MZILA: I don't know.....

QAMA: Come on Tony, we have be to honest with each other if we are to beat this!

MZILA: the girl, the actress!

QAMA: Thandeka...

MZILA: Yes, she stopped by and I made a sandwich for her after the policemen had ordered.

QAMA: So you refused to do their order..

MZILA: Moreoless, the bottom line is that the bastards are not welcome in my café.

QAMA: But this is South Africa you know that – we cannot as blacks pick and chose who we serve.

MZILA: ...I know...

QAMA: Then why, you could have just walked away.

MZILA: (thinking): You know what Ned, I saw you as a baby growing up and now as a youngman, throughout my life I have seen disrespect and more disrespect. I am 56 years old and you are 31. For 56 years I have carried this thing in my heart!

QAMA: What thing....

MZILA: The burden of being a second class citizen; I have heard enough, all this money means absolutely nothing to me, I have heard it.

QAMA: We all have heard it but this is not the way to go, we cannot go bound for bound with them

MZILA: I know, but those two bastards kept on pushing and pushing (song)...

[We push push...]

QAMA: Pushing and pushing.....

MZILA: They don't have a case unless.. (whispering)

QAMA: Unless they find those papers, you are thinking what I am thing; where did you put the papers.

MZILA: Take a guess...

QAMA: I don't have time for that, all I know is that if they find those papers, you are in serious trouble, so am I and the other members of the congress, so where did you put them.

MZILA: (motions to the coffee maker)...In the coffee maker!

QAMA: Coffee maker!!! Tony, of all places.

MZILA:....and that's why I could not make them their coffee and toast! Get it.

QAMA: They have a warrant to search the place in the next thirty minutes, I got to go...

MZILA: Run *mfana (boy)* run...... (song)

ACT III: SCENE I

The two police officers enter, Runseen and Cronje, they approach TONY's café.

RUNSEEN: We got him now; let's gather enough information and we will have a guilty conviction by tomorrow night. I warned him but he would not listen. Bloody kaffir!

CRONJE: They never listen these people – South Africa is not their country. We built this county from the ground; their country was just sticks and dirt. The white man built this country.

RUNSEEN: Trey telling that to the ANC –

CRONJE: I know, where should we begin --- the search?

RUNSEEN: Let's work our way to the center of the café. East meets west.

The search starts and then moments later -

CRONJE: Ya, Janie, Do you think we could have handled this differently, I mean, this is the man's café. It's like coming into his home –

RUBNSEEN: Sometimes I wonder about you, are you going soft – a leftie perhaps. We have to come down hard like a hammer on these people.

CRONJE: But why so hard, are we not a Christian nation after all!

RUNSEEEN: Christian nation your ass – the Bible is rather clear on who is the master and the slave. The whites are a Christian nation not the blacks.

CRONJE: where does it say this...

RUNSEEN: Some where in the old testament.

CRONJE: Not New! I thought you had said new previously.

RUNSEEN: No I am mistaken, the new testament, I think Jesus put the matter to rest once and for all. New and old does it really matter Janie.

CRONJE: That's funny,... I was a Reformed advent church goer school, I don't recall such a conversation?

RUNSEEN: maybe you skipped the part when Jesus discusses who is on top.

CRONJE: (shaking his head) Or maybe you made it all up! Ya, Janie!

RUNSEEN: Look Cronje, I saw how you looked at that girl this morning, ..I am still a rank above you ...now lets get back to work...no more politics. We are here for Vorstrekker, no more political side talk. Our grandfathers did not die for Bantu rule Janie.

CRONJE: But our laws are now politics.

RUNSEEN: I don't care chana, don't care what the philosophy is about our laws; the only thing I am clear about is that blacks and whites are not equal. Even God knows this!

CRONJE: maybe there are two Gods, one for the whites and one for blacks! One in the Bible and another in politics.

RUNSEEN: Shut you...just shut up, ya. You talk too much.

CRONJE: All..I.

RUNSEEN: Just get back to work, no more Bantu power ya!

Moments later....

CRONJE: By the way what are we looking for?

RUNSEEN: You are starting to annoy me chana, how can you execute a search warrant and not know what you are looking for.

CRONJE: We usually just search for everything and anything.

RUNBSEEN (annoyed): Here is the warrant, read it yourself.

CRONJE: (Reading aloud)Warrant for search signed Woodward: In the case against Tony Mzila, permission to search for coffee maker and toast maker as evidence in case.

(stops)..in that case I have the toast maker right here (pointing) and all we need is the toast maker!

RUNSEEN: Good Cronje, lets' keep looking....

The two bury into the café...

RUNSEEN: Nothing....are we missing any thing.

CRONJE: Nope...what..about

RUNSEEN: What...

CRONJE: No ...

RUNSEEN: Speak Cronje, do you know that you have a tendency of not speaking your mind.

CRONJE: What about the top counter.

RUNSEEN: Good...lets look at those then we are done, if the poor bugger did not have a coffee maker he should have said no. Maybe the poor fellow was embarrassed!

CRONJE: Funny these things...

RUNSEEN: Keep looking Cronje..

As the two men get ready to climb to the top counters, enter **THANDILE DANZILE**, the actress.

THANDILE: Good afternoon officers.

CRONJE: (stops in mid air).Good afternoon!

RUNSEEN: Concentrate chana...

CRONJE: How is everything in the play world..

THANDEKA: Very demanding..

CRONJE: What play now?

THANDEKA: Richard, the III.

CRONJE: Interesting, now tell me why Shakespeare in South Africa.

Thandeka: Why not?

CRONJE: It would appear to be misplaced, don't you have any African playwrights, or black American – Shakespeare, and the man is a white Englishman, what benefit could possibly come from doing a play by a white man.

THANDEKA: Its not the color of the writer that determines of the play is good or bad, it's the writing itself-

CRONJE: How so...

THANDEKA: Even if Shakespeare were black that does not mean white people should not perform his plays. A play is a work of art, independent of political persuasions, it transcends the current politics. It is the artist's mission – writer – to transcend the racial divide. We find in Shakespeare themes that persist in our community... here in South Africa.

CRONJE: But Richard the III. That's about a man obsessed with power.

THANDEKA: That's a play that can be seen as a South African tale as well.....our leaders and king Richard share something in common...

CRONJE: And that is what!

THANDEKA: They are like King Richard, -- that is Prime Minister Malan. will give anything to be in power!

RUNSEEN: Careful....are you rocking the boat? Politics, does this café attract the most political active Bantu yet.

CRONJE: No ..Jack, she is just explaining her play Richard the III.

RUNSEEN: What does a Bantu woman know about Shakespeare! Nothing

CRONJE: Come on Runseen, no need for all that...she is a lovely lady.

RUNSEEN: Lovely or not –get back to work and that's an order Johnny!

As **JOHHNY CRONJE** returns to the café, **NED QAMA** enters, huffing and puffing his way in.

NED QAMA: Afternoon gentlemen.

CRONJE: Yes attorney Qama, ...you obviously know this is a crime scene..

NED QAMA: yes, and gentlemen I am exercising <u>section 2:16</u> of the criminal justice act. My right to watch the search in action. Here is the order signed by Woodward.

RUNSEEN: Let me see.....okay...seems to be in order. Okay, keep your distance and you will be okay. Now where were we...too many disturbances....Cronje your black beauty has got to go and Qama maintain working distance please.

CRONJE: There is no need to be rude..

RUNSEEN: When we get to the station please remind me to write you up for insubordination...you are taking sides with the blacks against us. Remember where your bread is buttered...COMRADE!

CRONJE: You heard him folks, this is a crime scene...

Just as the two police offers prepare to resume their search...

THANDEKA: (To Cronje) Will you come and see the play..

RUNSEEN (infuriated): No...Johnny you know that blacks and whites cannot be in the same building unless there is prior approval by State department...No, he is not going to see you in Richard the III.

CRONJE: I will see.

RUNSEEN: Just go and I will have you badge. This one (shakes head).

Ned seizes the moment to dash to the upper counters, as the officers turn – they miss NED as he runs out with the coffee maker.

RUNSEEN: How, something strange, ..what happened to that that talkative **QAMA**.

THANDEKA: I saw him leave, he said by while we were talking.

RUNSEEN: That's fishy, I smell a rat..

CRONJE: (ironically) and I smell nothing...

RUNSEEN: We will need to interview that NED fellow later..

CRONJE: For what?

RUNSEEN: Obstruction of justice!

CRONJE: maybe we should indict the whole town for obstruction of justice...

RUNSEEN: very funny, remind me to write you up when we get to the police station..

CRONJE: I will definitely do that.

The two men stare at each other, there is a new sense of enmity between them.

RUNSEEN: And to think, I am the one who recommended your skinny self for corporal, I should have listened to what they were saying about you...my bleeding heart friend. You are the reason why we have not been effectively able to deal with blacks in this country. And another thing...your girlfriend is obstructing justice, she should leave in the next two minutes, no make that two seconds...

Thandeka rushes out...

CRONJE: Bye Thandie...

THANDEKA: Bye Johny...

RUNSEEN: the two of you make me sick, you Cronje are rocking the boat my friend..simply rocking the boat.

THANDEKA AND CRONJE: what boat!

Thandeka exists, leaving the two men to search the café.

ACT III SCENE II

The court room is a somber and dry atmosphere, Dickenson yet perfunctory.
    Enter TONY, from one end and Pienaar from another end. MAGISTRATE
    WOODWARD, JOSEPHINE WOODWARD, awaits both parties at the
    center. The atmosphere is thick!

One side is the State with the two police officers and on the other is the
    defendant, gingerly eager to clear his name.

Voice off stage: all rise...

and the knocking of provincial bureaucracy.

MAGISTRATE WOODWARD speaks delicately.

MAGISTARTE JOSEPHINE: In the Matter of **State v. MZILA**, having entered a
plea of not guilty we will proceed to hear the evidence. Mr.Mzila, having been
and entered appearance through attorney at law, Ned Qama, understands the
full implications of these charges. The charge of treason against by the State
carries with it a life sentence. Mr. Mzila do you understand these charges.

NED whispers to **TONY.**

TONY: Yes.

MAGISTRATE WOODWARD: DO you understand that if found guilty, you face prison time.

TONY MZILA: Yes

MAGISTRATE WOODWARD: very well, then let's proceed. Mr. Pienaar you represent the State in this case, please begin your case.

PIENAAR: Thank you your honor.

MAGISTRATE WOODWARD: Opening arguments please...

PIENAAR: Two days ago, Mr. Tony Mzila, a local café owner living in the Bantu township in Simon's Town Capetown was arrested and charged super-intending, under the new laws and more specifically under the Sedition Act. He is charged under section 2:116 of the Sedition Act for acting in such a way as to pervert the interests of the State.

He categorically refused to serve the two police offers coffee and toast, and under the statute – treason – is any act against State action; since police represent State action – he so properly charged.

MAGISTARTE WOODWARD: Mr. Pienaar, are we to assume that every police action is also State action.

PIENAAR: Yes.

MAGISTARTE WOODWARD: Even illegal acts?

PIENAAR: Your honor with all due respect I are am not finished.

MAGISTARTE WOODWARD: Continue, Mr. Pienaar.

PIENAAR: The State is not saying the police are immune to illegality or above the law; the State is simply saying in this case and in this case only; we allude to the fact that the actions of the two police officer, two days ago – were State action.

MAGISTARTE WOODWARD: The request for coffee and toast is State action?

PIENAAR: Yes, so far as this is tied in with surveillance and a methodological investigative case. And cooperation of persons with ongoing investigations.

MAGISTARTE WOODWARD: Was MR. Mzila, under investigation?

PIENAAR: Yes...

MAGISTRATE WOODWARD: For what...

PIENAAR: Seditious Acts and in support of terrorism.

MAGISTRATE WOODWARD: But Mr. Pienaar, even he was under investigation, why arrest him for something that seems a stretch to your investigation. The refusal to serve the two police officers.

PIENAAR: Your honor, our case is piecemeal and this is one of the peaces. The refusal to serve is tied in with a pre-emptive cover up.

MAGISATRATE WOODWARD: So you do not have any independent collaborative evidence of this Sedition you so eloquently speak off.

PIENAAR: No, the investigation has not concluded.

MAGISTRATE WOODWARD: Okay, Pienaar is that all.

PIENAAR: Yes, thank you, your honor.

MAGISTRATE WOODARD: Mr. QAMA, you may State your case.

QAMA: My client, Ned Qama, owners the café Tony's Café and was arrested on March 16th 1948; the short end of the stick is that his refusal to serve the two police officers coffee and toast is not Sedition. Our position is entirely a legal one; no way in the statute is there a definition of Sedition as failure to serve police officers their meals. The act must clearly State what State action is and what not State action is. If the State would like to include these definitions, then it should be a legislative process and not a judicial interpretation by the PIENAAR. The act is too ambiguous and such Mr. Mzila must be found to have acted outside of what the Act criminalizes, unless something else – some imprimatur of evidence is found to act in corroboration to the evidence in chief. I cite Republic of South Africa v. Mothsmayi.

MAGISTRATE WOODWARD: Let me get this right, are you saying people can refuse to comply with police orders?

QAMA: Yes, if those orders have no value on the direct duties of police officers. Here, what we see, are two police officers trying to bully a man to serve them in his own café in their own spare time and hiding under the Seditious Act.

PIENAAR: We object to that tone of voice.

MAGISATRE WOODWARD: Overruled.

PIENAAR: Your owner.

MAGISATRATE WOODWARD: I am the judge here Mr. Pienaar, Mr. Qama is entitled to his opening Statement.

QAMA: Our position is that the police officers cannot use the State's legislation to ask for prompt and fast service; we also offer your honor the fact that there is no evidence that Ned Qama refused to serve the officers. The officers concluded, wrongly - as the evidence will show - that delay in their order was a refusal.

Our position is that even if your honor concludes --- and the case law argues against this, State v. Motsamayi, and State v. Botha --- that the order to serve toast and coffee is not State action, then our super-intending position is that Tony never refused at all. He simply made a human refusal. The two issues are whether –

a. Orders by police officers for meals and snacks are State action ---

b. And whether Tony refused these orders. If the State finds in the negative on all these questions then the defendant is innocent, and in the alternative if your honor finds in the negative on any question – the inconsistency between the first part and second part argues for the defendant's innocence. Thank you your honor.

MAGISTRATE WOODWARD: Thank you Mr. Qama; Mr. Pienaar you may begin with your testimony.

PIENAAR: Your honor, with all due respect the State would like to ask that you recuse yourself from this case.

MAGISTRATE WOODWARD: No way Mr. Pienaar, please proceed with your testimony, I have no intention of recusing myself!

PIENAAR: The State wishes to call JACK RUNSEEN!

Mr. Jack Runseen stumbles to the dock.

MAGISTRATE WOODWARD: (Looking yonder) Do you swear to tell the truth nothing but the truth so help you God.

RUNSEEN: I swear your honor.

MAGISTRATE WOODWARD: Very good, proceed Mr. Pienaar.

PIENAAR: Please tell the court what happened on the day of April 1948.

QAMA: I object, foundation?

MAGISRATE: Sustained. Mr. Pienaar please establish the officer's profession and duty on that day.

PIENAAR: Mr. Runseen, what is your current profession?

RUNSEEN: I am a police officer with the South African Police department, and have help this position for ten years.

PIENAAR: Okay, now what is your duty?

RUNSEEN: I am a patrol officer, operation on second and Third Street in Simon's Town.

PIENAAR: Are you familiar with the defendant?

RUNSEEN: Yes, he was arrested for seditious infraction.

PIENAAR: Please explain to the court.

RUNSEEN: Under the new law, a person cannot distribute material that is a protest to the new system.

PIENAAR: Let's go to this business of the coffee.

RUNSEEN: We believe that the owner, this Mzila fellow was hiding something and that this was all a secret and elaborate cover up.

PIENAAR: Why do you assume this?

QAMA: Objection, speculation, call for argument.

MAGISTRATE WOODWARD: Very good Qama, I will allow this, let me hear what the man might do.

RUNSEEN: We find that the Bantu has developed very imaginative and intelligent ways to disseminate information. And an unidentified informer told us that this Mzila is part of the underground anti-Apartheid movement.

PIENAAR: So you have reason that this denial of coffee and toast was just a ruse.

RUNSEEN: Yes, clearly he is hiding something.

MAGISTRATE WOODWARD: Any further questions Mr. Pienaar?

PIENAAR: Your honor, no.

MAGISTRATE WOODWARD: Is this your only evidence? (Shaking head)

PIENAAR: Yes, very much so.

MAGISTRATE WOODWARD: Your cross Qama.

QAMA: Thank you your honor. Mr. Runseen, was a toaster and coffee maker recovered?

RUNSEEN: No, just the toaster.

PIENAAR: Objection.

MAGISTRATE WOODWARD: Grounds.

PIENAAR: I object to this Bantu questioning in this manner.

MAGISTRATE WOODWARD: Overruled.

QAMA: Okay, so an informer led you to Mr. Mzila.

RUNSEEN: Yes.

QAMA: Do you have independent collaboration of this informer.

RUNSEEN: No.

QAMA: What of the coffee maker, did you find it?

RUNSEEN: No

QAMA: No further questions, your honor I respectfully submit that this case be thrown out for lack of evidence.

MAGISTRATE WOODWARD: Mr. Pienaar.

PIENAAR: The State has met its burden and it is beyond a reasonable doubt here, that Mr. Mzila had seditious material.

MAGISTARTE WOODWARD: I disagree; I am throwing this one out Mr. Pienaar. The evidence is not conclusive. A man refuses to serve two police officers. An unidentified informer. Just not enough.

(Banging hammer) Mr. **Mzila** you may go home.

ACT II SCENE III

Darkness on stage and actors are illumined.

15 years later. Rivonia

The judge now fifteen years older sits. Looking tired and beat down by Apartheid. The man is not Mzila, but the thread is familiar. A man in his mid-forties is in now in the dock

NELSON MANDELA: ....During my lifetime I have dedicated myself to this struggle of the African people. I have fought against white domination, and I have fought against black domination.

I have cherished the ideal of a democratic and free society in which all persons live together in harmony and with equal opportunities. It is an ideal which I hope to live for and to achieve. But if needs be, it is an ideal for which I am prepared to die. (Mandela, 1963, Rivonia Trial)

(Drum roll)

Curtains roll....Song plays in:

Dedicated to Malandela kaLuzumana,

King of the Nguni

Finnis

The Tragic Circumstances of 1948

A Play by Ken Sibanda

KEN SIBANDA's **TRAGIC CICUMSTANCES OF 1948** is the story of a South African café owner Tony Mzila who refuses to serve two racist police officers coffee and toast in his café. He is increasingly dragged into a deeper and hateful understanding of the new country under the draconian government of 1948.

www.ingramcontent.com/pod-product-compliance
Lightning Source LLC
Chambersburg PA
CBHW030307030426
42337CB00012B/626